SAFE HOUSE

Lydia Stryk

BROADWAY PLAY PUBLISHING INC
New York
www.broadwayplaypublishing.com
info@broadwayplaypublishing.com

SAFE HOUSE
© Copyright 2023 Lydia Stryk

First edition: November 2023
I S B N: 978-0-88145-993-7

Book design: Marie Donovan
Page make-up: Adobe InDesign
Typeface: Palatino

CHARACTERS & SETTING

HENRY, *an Intelligence Officer in the Department of Defense.*

MARY, HENRY'*s wife.*

MARTA, *a cultural attaché from elsewhere.*

The contemporary world.

A living room in HENRY *and* MARY'*s house, a bedroom, a study. A café. A meeting room. An unknowable site in another country.*

AUTHOR'S NOTES

The text makes use of ellipses and line breaks.
These represent thoughts that trail off or are held
momentarily; hesitation, suggestion, unspoken
meaning. Where literal pauses are noted, a little more
time is required. These directions are not meant to stop
the forward momentum of the plot.

The design team is urged to place the scenes in the
literal world, even if it is through image projection, and
to avoid abstraction. The play is set in the real world
and needs signposts.

The three characters might always be present.

There is room for humor in the play, in the character
of Henry, in particular—his antics, his word and
whistling choices. Please don't be afraid of it. Laughter
brings relief for the audience. Sometimes things are
funny until they're not funny, at all.

Henry's whistling melodies should be taken from
popular tunes now in the public domain.

SAFE HOUSE was inspired by the Robert Hanssen and
Aldrich Ames espionage cases and very loosely based
on certain details of their lives. I was most intrigued by
the role of their wives—their possible complicity but
also subversion. Intelligence exists through facade and
charade, a deadly form of theatre. Related is the role
of 'art' in the state apparatus embodied in the figure
of the cultural attaché. Preparing for the publication

of this play, I have been struck by the recent deaths in prison of a few notorious moles, including Hanssen. In times of peace, we tend to forget about them, but balanced on the precipice of another world war and an intensifying cold one, it is worth noting that there are moles burrowing within our institutions to this day and always will be as long as humans remain on the planet.

SAFE HOUSE is dedicated to my beloved friends in the acting profession.

And to Stanley Kauffmann, in memory.

Scene

(*A living room.* HENRY, MARY *and* MARTA)

HENRY: Well, it's been a good, safe place to raise a family. We've been happy with it, wouldn't you say? ...Mary?

MARY: The gates are manned twenty-four hours.

MARTA: Twenty-four!

MARY: The hardest part is getting out.

MARTA: Really?

HENRY: What Mary means is. She's been kept pretty much at home. Raising six boys—

MARTA: Six?

HENRY: That's right. Six young men, now.

MARY: (*Ignoring him*) If you don't belong. The guards will hold you at the gate. 'Til someone comes to vouch for you.

MARTA: Perhaps they'll hold me here!

MARY: Safe inside. With us.

(MARY *and* MARTA *laugh.*)

HENRY: You came with me. You're registered.

MARY: You're videoed!

MARTA: Oh, dear!

HENRY: Nothing to fear.

MARY: I used to play a game with them.

HENRY: Mary—

MARTA: —And which was that?

MARY: I'd play like I was someone else.

MARTA: And how?

MARY: Oh. I'd give another name, a false address.

MARTA: They let you out?

MARY: Yes. Every time.

MARTA: So the system has its cracks.

HENRY: They know you, Mary, after twenty-odd years.

MARY: Nothing's secure. When you want to get through…

MARTA: You do.

MARY: You do. *(A pause)* How long will you be staying here?

MARTA: In the cultural field, that's never clear…

MARY: I hope for a while?

MARTA: Me, too. It's such a fascinating city.

MARY: The artistic life is wide and varied.

HENRY: *(Getting up)* So…Mary?

MARY: Yes, dinner is ready.

(MARY and MARTA get up. They all start to move to another part of the house. HENRY goes first.)

MARY: Marta?

MARTA: *(Stopping)* Mary?

MARY: I'm so glad you came.

MARTA: Thank you! I am, too!

MARY: And I hope I'll see you again—

(HENRY comes back in to the room. MARY and MARTA turn sharply to face him.)

(End of scene)

Scene

(MARY *and* HENRY *in bed. He is sleeping.*)

MARY: I've been thinking, Henry, about the cultural attaché. *(She looks at him, noting that he is fast asleep.)* I think she might be dangerous.

For us, I mean.

We're a close-knit family unit. On secure financial footing. With good credit. We live in a beautiful house. And it's all paid up. And you work tirelessly at the agency.

(HENRY *yells out in his sleep, winces.*)

MARY: Things are exactly the way they should be. And how they seem.

(End of scene)

Scene

(*A busy café in the heart of the city.* MARY *and* MARTA)

MARY: What does a cultural attaché do? Exactly?

MARTA: That's a good question. There are several answers. One is easy.

(MARTA *smiles broadly,* MARY *leans in.*)

MARTA: We bring our culture here to you. And send yours back.
But a culture is a funny thing. It can't really be grasped, in truth, from someone outside it. Oh, we cast our shadows back and forth. In blinding color. But my being here is politics. The art and dance of peace and war. It keeps things fluid between us.

MARY: Henry meets a lot of people. They all have functions. And they never stay for long. Each one speaks our language in a different melody. Like instruments in a gorgeous symphony.

MARTA: Hmm. What instrument am I?

MARY: You. You're…a harp.

MARTA: I'm flattered.
I hear voices so differently. Crossed lines. And a great deal of static.

(MARY *looks startled,* MARTA *smiles.*)

MARTA: Of course, I hear music, too. And poetry.
My father was a poet. And my mother, she was a poet, too. And my grandfather was a poet. And his father before him. And both of my brothers are in the literary field. One, god forgive him, is a critic. The other, a scholar of ancient texts. I have a sister—

MARY: A sister!

MARTA: She's my twin.

MARY: How wonderful that must have been.

MARTA: She was a poet, too. In spirit. But she's no longer…
She disappeared.

MARY: No…

MARTA: She was gentle, soft. She lived for her art. And her art, alone. She believed in beauty and found it everywhere. And the beauty of truth. She heard the world much like you.

MARY: What was her name?

MARTA: *(A pause)* Marta.

MARY: …Oh, I get it! *(She studies* MARTA *triumphantly.)* You *are* a poet. You're a poet, but you're something else as well. A painter? A dancer. No, I don't think so. I think you're an actress.

MARTA: I *was* an actress.

MARY: I knew it! I knew.

MARTA: A very bad actress.

MARY: I don't believe that.

MARTA: It's sadly true.

MARY: You're so charismatic. Expressive and mysterious—

MARTA: *(Laughing)* —Stop, please stop!

MARY: You could be from anywhere!

MARTA: Anywhere?

MARY: *(Catching herself, embarrassed)* Well, other than *here.*

MARTA: Everywhere. And in between?

MARY: You could play any part. Is what I mean.

MARTA: I studied with a famous Russian teacher in Paris. She told me, "Marta, it's all very dramatic. But it won't do. You are acting for Hecuba."

MARY: For "Hecuba"?

MARTA: I was acting for the Gods. And not in the scene. Acting up a storm. Without any truth.

MARY: But acting isn't true. It's acting!

MARTA: Oh, no. On the contrary. The finest acting is completely truthful. The actor believes in what she is doing. While it is happening, of course. Completely.

MARY: (Slowly) I played the mother's part for over half my life. But I never believed in it completely. The words I spoke seemed to come from somewhere else. Outside of me. It never felt completely real. Maybe life is only real on stage.

MARTA: What part would you most like to play?

MARY: Oh, that's a tough one. You see…

MARTA: Go on.

MARY: I never allowed myself the luxury. Of imagining another life.

MARTA: I don't believe that.

MARY: (A pause) Henry was sent abroad. Just recently. And with the boys gone, I went along. It was a whirlwind tour, starting in Jerusalem. And then further on to Ashgabat. Kabul. Islamabad. Baghdad, Cairo. And in Mecca, our tour ended. And somewhere along that extraordinary route. My handbag was stolen. And among other things, both valuable and worthless, I lost my passport. And now, I often wonder about it. Someone stole it. And then someone must have bought it. And somewhere a woman is using my identity. She robbed me of it.

MARTA: *(Lightly)* Losing one's identity is not such a tragedy.

MARY: I wonder where she went with it. And what she is doing. And who she was before she became me. And if she misses herself. I hope she embarked on a marvelous journey…
and became exactly who she wanted to be
for both of us.
I can't get over that we bumped into each other.

MARTA: Chance. Fate. Mystery.

MARY: I'll take all three.

MARTA: What time are you meeting Henry?

MARY: At four. Every Saturday…

MARTA: He meets you here?

MARY: Well, I like to shop. And so we've worked this out. He does errands of some sort. I don't ask what—

MARTA: No.

(MARY *and* MARTA *laugh in recognition.*)

MARY: —and then he picks me up. Because I don't like driving in the city.
I shop. And then I stop in here. And wait for him.

MARTA: Every Saturday.

MARY: Without fail. You would find me.
If you wanted to.

(End of scene)

Scene

(A meeting room. There is a window with drawn curtains. MARTA and HENRY sit facing each other.)

MARTA: I need to thank you for arranging my trip.

HENRY: Only too happy to have been of help.

MARTA: And for clearing up the problems with the paperwork.

HENRY: Sometimes solutions are unorthodox.

MARTA: Coming into the country as your wife!

HENRY: Well, we want to help you make a new life.

(MARTA takes a passport out of her purse and slides it across the table. HENRY takes it and slips it into his pocket.)

HENRY: A fresh start.

MARTA: Start, yes.

HENRY: Without the burden of those secrets you keep. We'll take them.

(There is a pause. MARTA looks away, draws a sharp breath. She turns back to HENRY.)

MARTA: *(Lightly)* Your wife is a lovely woman.

HENRY: She can talk your ear off about the boys. And the rennovation of our kitchen.

MARTA: I look forward to meeting her again.

HENRY: She likes to shop in the city. But she doesn't like to drive. It scares her. So I take her in. And drop her off. And pick her up later at her favorite café. It's funny the people she bumps into there. You'd be surprised.

MARTA: *(Slowly)* Well, when you sit still, the world comes to you.

HENRY: Maybe you could meet her there one day. I'm sure she would enjoy your company. *(A pause)* The menu caters to everyone's taste. Whatever you order, you can't go wrong. But you have to make a decision. And fairly quickly. Because they do get busy. And if you miss the opportunity, they move on. And then there's no guarantee that there'll be anything left. People here are very hungry.

MARTA: Heat takes away the appetite.

HENRY: It's a matter of degree. You can see it two ways. It's a chance and there's no other choice.

(A pause)

MARTA: One adjusts to the climate.

HENRY: That's more like it.
Although there are some poor suckers who never do. The heat kills them. They disappear in it. They just can't stick it. One fellow I knew melted clean away. A marathon runner! One poor gal burnt to a crisp. Terrible. Smoke pouring out of her ears, her nostrils. Well, that's why we have Antarctica, Siberia—or Minnesota, for that matter. For people like that. *(He slides a card across the table to her.)* This place is a good safe bet. When it comes to what you're looking for.

(MARTA takes it and slips it in her purse.)

HENRY: Why don't you call and make an appointment? The highways here can be problematic, but there are safer routes, depending on the weather. Some faster, some slower.

(End of scene)

Scene

(MARY *and* HENRY *in bed. He is sleeping.*)

MARY: It's funny, Henry. I'm still dreaming peace-time things. As if there was. Being late to pick the kids up. Waiting at the wrong bus stop. I dreamed that one of the boys was homosexual. And I expect he is, don't you? They say one in ten are. Why not Henry, Jr.? Then suddenly, I was holding the cultural attaché. In my arms!
But then you woke me with one of your cries.

(HENRY *cries out in his sleep, waking himself.* MARY *pretends to sleep. He checks to see if she is sleeping and satisfied, gets out of bed. He dresses himself, always checking to make sure he is not disturbing her sleep. Then he goes out and closes the door behind him. She sits up.*)

MARY: There is no such thing as nine-to-five in the life of an officer of the government. Enemies work around the clock. He must be ready at any time. And he is sworn to secrecy. Even when it comes to his own family. The Oath of Office is a sacred trust.

(*End of scene*)

Scene

(A study. HENRY, alone. He speaks into a microcassette recorder. A package wrapped in a plastic bag, newspaper, scotch tape and a second plastic bag sit on the desk.)

HENRY: Dear Friends. Your appreciation means the world to me. And I am sorry for the delay in my response. Age, they say, brings wisdom. It also brings new worries and a need for caution. Large bills associated with the renovation of our kitchen. Winds of change blowing through the Institution. But, please rest assured that you are not forgotten. You remain in my thoughts, as you will ascertain.
I've put together some materials over the course of several months. Some of it urgent. The rest I hope instructive.
Yours in friendship… *(A pause)* Clark Kent.

(HENRY stops the recorder. He hits the rewind button, then play, listening to his words. He removes the microcassette tape and gently wraps it in a tiny piece of newspaper and tapes it up and slips it into the bag containing the package, whistling innocuously as he works. He tapes the bag closed tightly and places it in a second plastic bag. He dresses himself to go outside, then switches off the light. Whichever cheery recognizable melody he is whistling might be repeated over the course of the play. Or perhaps there is a playlist of melodies in his head.)

(End of scene)

Scene

(MARY *and* MARTA *at the café.*)

MARY: Sometimes I lose control.

MARTA: Oh?

MARY: I throw things...

MARTA: What kind of things?

MARY: Soft things.

MARTA: Well, then.

MARY: Pillows, socks...

MARTA: Hardly counts.

MARY: And I scream.

MARTA: Not out loud!?

MARY: You know me already, I see. Silently. I scream to myself, and I say...

MARTA: What do you say?

MARY: Oh, terrible things...

MARTA: ...Like?

MARY: "I hate you." "I can't stand the sight of you." "I want to kill you."

MARTA: Oh, you mean, the usual.

MARY: Have you ever felt like killing someone?

MARTA: Your question presupposes that I never have.

MARY: Have you?!

MARTA: Not with my bare hands.

MARY: Oh, well then...

MARTA: Of course not. Don't look so askance. Well, not *directly*. But we're all responsible for somebody's death. We're all implicated. And, yes.

MARY: Yes?

MARTA: I have wanted to kill someone.

MARY: It's hard to admit it.

MARTA: It's human. When you're trapped, you want to strike back.

MARY: Henry is a decent man.
He plays the clown at children's parties.

MARTA: Astonishing! And charming.

MARY: *(Suddenly)* I'm not happy, Marta. …I wish I knew the secret to happiness.

MARTA: The secret to happiness…

MARY: Go on.

MARTA: What a funny phrase that is. Because what is a secret?

MARY: I'm telling secrets now.

MARTA: Are they secrets, really?

MARY: I think so…

MARTA: But I knew them already. Your unhappiness is no secret, Mary. *(A pause)* The secret is…that there are no secrets. But then you knew that. *(Pause)* A secret. Now, that would be a revelation that could change the world. But it's the same old world.

MARY: No secrets.

MARTA: We play like there are, of course. Because we can't bear

MARY: knowing

MARTA: what we know.

There's a children's game where I come from. Someone has a secret and passes it on. It gets passed on from ear to ear. And the secret is never what it started out to be. By the end, it's the opposite of what it was.

MARY: Henry asked me how my day in town went. What I saw. Who I met. I didn't tell him I met you.

MARTA: Oh. Why not?

MARY: It felt right.

MARTA: Will you tell him that we met today?

MARY: No. If you don't mind. I'd like to keep it...

MARTA: Secret?

(MARY *nods,* MARTA *and* MARY *laugh.*)

MARTA: All right.

(*End of scene*)

Scene

(The meeting room. HENRY *and* MARTA*)*

HENRY: Now that you're settled into your new post. It's high time you explored the area.

MARTA: And what do you recommend I see here?

HENRY: There's a patch of forest I like to visit. Well, it's near the house, so it's convenient. The vistas are to die for. But you have to keep your eyes open. Some dodos get lost. Head in the clouds. Never come out. The bears eat 'em.

MARTA: Sounds delightful.

HENRY: The sign says "Welcome to the woods. This way to the camping grounds." Lovers have their trysts there and leave each other notes on the signal post. There's a small wooden bridge over a rocky stream near a trash container in a wooden shed. *(He slides a piece of paper across to her.)* Here's a map of the area. Should you ever want to go there.

*(*MARTA *takes it and puts it in her purse.)*

HENRY: Timing is everything. I tend to walk at night. It's dangerous for women alone, of course. They jog or walk their dogs at dawn…
The weather should be excellent next week. If you feel like a stroll. Think back three months ago. How cold it was. And three days from now, how warm it will be.

(End of scene)

Scene

(HENRY, alone. He speaks into the recorder, newspaper, scotch tape and plastic bag by his side.)

HENRY: Dear Friends. I am pleased to hear that your curiosity is being satisfied. And the diamonds are much appreciated. How they sparkle on my wife's neck.

I think you will find the enclosed quite useful. Though I hope you will never have cause to use it. *(He laughs uncomfortably, and then grows confident again.)* Payment in cash is again acceptable. And this time, given my position, quite desirable.

Yours as ever... *(A pause)* The Lone Ranger. *(He stops the recorder, removes the tape, makes his package and leaves, whistling all the while.)*

(End of scene)

Scene

(MARY *and* MARTA. MARY *wears a diamond necklace.*)

MARY: There's more…

MARTA: Are you sure you want to …?

MARY: (*She nods, continues.*) He shouts out in his sleep. He shakes. He winces under terrible blows.

MARTA: And you don't know what—

MARY: No.

MARTA: You don't know why—

MARY: He never tells me anything. That's how it's always been.

MARTA: I see… And why did you marry him?

MARY: My mother liked him.

(MARY *shrugs.* MARTA *and* MARY *begin to laugh. Their laughter grows almost raucous.*)

MARY: He adores the boys and he's been a good husband. And he's an excellent provider. I've wanted for nothing, except….

MARTA: Except?

MARY: There's something empty at the center of him. I used to think that I could fill it. It even excited me to enter it.

MARTA: And now?

MARY: That's over.

MARTA: And yet you stay—

MARY: Well, marriage is a sacred vow.

MARTA: I knew a pair under the old regime. The
loveliest couple. Everybody thought so. Artistic
and sensitive, both active in the struggle. He was
a schoolteacher. She played the piano. But she was
harassed over the years, and finally lost her job in the
symphony. Her husband supported her and always
found a way to rescue her from greater harm. But she
ended up in prison eventually despite his loving care.
Oh, he visited her there religiously and fought very
publicly to win her release, which in the end, he did.
But she was broken by it. And never played again.
Shunned from all sides, her husband was her only
friend.

MARY: She was lucky to have him.

MARTA: When the secret service files were opened.
After the regime collapsed. She discovered that the
person who had spied on her and betrayed her all
those years? Well, it was none other than.

MARY: Surely not.

MARTA: I'm afraid so. Although he used a code
name. Everyone did who worked for them. She knew
immediately that it was him. No one else knew the
things about her that the regime used against her.

(MARY *looks away, distressed.*)

MARTA: He later confessed. Needless to say, that
marriage ended. (*She stops, and then quietly, begins to
recite 'The Song of Betrayal.'*)
Once in a blue moon
A man and woman fell in love
And in rapid succession
Told each other all their secrets
And vowed eternal devotion
In that order.

Well, it was a time of crisis
Breeding anguished desires
And intense declarations.
The ground under your feet
Was liable to shift
The roof over your head
The very bed—could vanish
Just like that.

Our two lovers
Suddenly discovered
The soft place in the center of their head
Because the hats they wore
Now covered skulls of the dead.

Let it suffice to say
That the secrets they kept
Soon found their way to others
Strangers, Big Brothers
They sold their secrets for money, honey
Chocolates and favors
Even of the neighbors.

And finally they sold the secrets of each other
 Without the other knowing
 But with the undergarments of their shame showing
 Red, like blood.

MARY: (*Shaking her head, forcefully*) That was no
marriage.

MARTA: Husbands betrayed their wives. Wives
betrayed their husbands. That happened, too. And
just as often. And both much more than you'd care to
imagine. It was far less common than sexual betrayal,
of course, but far more dangerous for the person
betrayed.
Still, for the betrayer, the rewards could be enormous.
(*A pause*) Betrayal is a funny thing.

MARY: Go on.

MARTA: I mean, what is it really? In itself, it's a thing
neither bad nor good. It all depends on who does what
and why someone tells it. On where you are standing.
Sometimes betrayal is the highest form of love.

MARY: Love?

MARTA: A love of truth, of what is right, of justice.
Betrayal for the sake of humanity. We call them heroes
and saints. But they are also betrayers. With love, you
always end up betraying. Somebody or something.
And then, of course, there is "love of country". An idea
whose good sense has always escaped me. Because
each regime is as corrupt as the other. And there are
very few, Mary, I have not lived under.
And we are all stuck here on this rather tiny planet.

MARY: But loyalty to one's country is a necessity.

MARTA: Is it, Mary, really? And why is that?

MARY: It's our only means of assuring our security.

MARTA: From where you are standing, I'm sure that's
true. Or, at least, you need to believe it's true.
Loyal to your country, disloyal to your spouse—

MARY: —I didn't mean I agreed with that!

MARTA: No, of course not. But that's where it leads
you.
Loyal to your spouse, disloyal to your country—

MARY: Please. This subject is uncomfortable for me—

MARTA: Is there anyone who is not a traitor? Sooner or
later. You betray another. Or yourself, for that matter.
Most people do that. They betray their principles,
promises, dreams, convictions. Their energy, talents,
intelligence. The past, future, the present moment. And
all this, before they get out of bed in the morning. And
then there are people for whom loyalty means nothing
as a concept. Betrayal by such a person is sometimes

the most shocking. It's not what you expect. They
betray betrayal, itself! In some ways, they are the most
honest among us.

MARY: I knew a woman exactly like that! She was a liar
through and through. The lies she told were... Well,
for her, I think, they weren't lies she told. Although, of
course, they *were*.
She spread stories that were irrational, fantastical.
She'd lie about what she read in the paper, seen on
TV. She'd lie about what you told her and what she
answered. In fact, I don't think she said a true thing.
Or if she did, it was an accident. But no one questioned
her, can you imagine? They accepted what she said
and followed where she led them.

MARTA: Like a leader in war time.

MARY: She was everyone's best friend. Including my
mother's.

MARTA: And was anyone the worse for it?

MARY: Not her, that's for sure. She lived to be a
hundred.

MARTA: Her lies sustained her. It's the truth that's
deadly.

MARY: Oh, she died several times. According to her, of
course. Of every kind of disorder.

(MARTA *and* MARY *laugh.*)

MARY: If she'd made chicken for dinner, she'd claim it
was a roast.

MARTA: Even if you'd eaten with her?

MARY: Oh, sure. She could shake your faith. Your five
senses.

MARTA: She was very talented!

MARY: ...And very self-assured.

MARTA: True to her nature.

MARY: And she liked especially to gain people's trust.

MARTA: Life is full of paradox.

MARY: Guess what her name was?

MARTA: Tell me.

MARY: Queenie. Queenie LaBute.

(MARTA *and* MARY *laugh raucously.*)

MARY: She worked for the government in the Security Division.

(MARTA *and* MARY *laugh raucously again.*)

MARY: And she taught Sunday school, if you can believe it.

MARTA: I wonder what those poor babies learned.

MARY: Maybe that hell is heaven. And heaven is hell.

MARTA: That's supposing there's a heaven.

MARY: *(Exhilarated)* Maybe we're in heaven now...

(*A short pause,* MARY's *eyes fixed on* MARTA's.)

MARY: *(Catching herself, blushing)* But back to marriage...

MARTA: Oh, marriage is all right. For as long as it lasts. You stay until the fire reaches your floor and then you jump.

MARY: In your experience?

MARTA: Yes, I've been married. To answer your question.

(MARTA *and* MARY *laugh.*)

MARY: But you don't like to talk about it.

MARTA: On the contrary. I've been in love many times. Marriage played a role. They came in all persuasions. None of them lasted. And yet, I carry them with me.

And I celebrate the possibility of love every day. But my life is bound up with the times. Revolutions and fault lines. Everything you tell me will be held for you and carried wherever I am taken. And that is how it's always been.
Well, you asked.

(MARTA *and* MARY *sit for a while.*)

MARY: I take it you've betrayed someone.

MARTA: Oh, I must have. Once or twice. And you?

MARY: Not that I know of.

MARTA: No, of course not. *(A pause)* I happen to be looking for someone to trust.

(MARTA *and* MARY *look at each other.*)

MARTA: To trust with my life.

(A long pause)

MARY: I feel odd things. So close to you…

MARTA: Go on.

MARY: But I don't know you. We've only just met, and yet…

MARTA: We've met before—

MARY: Have we?

MARTA: Long ago.

MARY: Where?

MARTA: In a past life, of course.

MARY: Oh. I see…

MARTA: Didn't we meet in the land of Egypt? Or was it later in Jerusalem?

(MARY *shrugs, helplessly*)

MARTA: And then we met again. On the Baltic Sea. On a Viking Ship, wasn't it?

(MARY *laughs*)

MARTA: Were we married once? Hmm. I wonder.

(MARY *is enjoying this.*)

MARTA: Or—fellow soldiers?

(MARY *shows signs of discomfort.*)

MARTA: Or were we, in fact, mortal enemies—

MARY: No!

MARTA: —stabbing each other through the heart in combat—

MARY: *(Quickly)* No. Never. No. Not that

MARTA: —or in the back?

(*A pause*)

MARY: *(Quietly)* Never. *(Determined)* We've never met before.
I would have remembered you.

MARTA: Alright then, no. But here we are! Look at me.

(MARY *does.*)

MARTA: Here I am.

MARY: Here we are.

MARTA: That's all there is.

MARY: I just need to know…I want to…know.

MARTA: What? What do you need, Mary? A map of me? Do you want to see my passport—

MARY: *(Appalled)* No. Of course not.

MARTA: What can I tell you? About me that you don't know already?

MARY: You're asking things of me, demanding—

MARTA: "Demanding"!

MARY: Things—that I've never…I don't know …

MARTA: It's not so painful. Is it? Not knowing? You just need to get used to it. In fact, they say, it's the highest form of intelligence.

MARY: I don't aim so high.

MARTA: *(Forcefully)* You should.
I'm sorry.

MARY: No, no. It's okay.

I know everything about the wives I meet. At brunches and state dinners. I know where their aches and pains are. Their large humiliations. When they're hungry. And what for. Their pet peeves. Their little joys. Their malicious victories. I know when they're about to drink that one too many. How many days they've been in AA. Bathroom habits. Prescription doses. Chemical sensitivities. I know what they want before they ask for it. Before they know, themselves.

MARTA: My, oh, my! You remind me of Madame Clairvue, the mind-reader. She was quite a beloved turn on the music-hall. Until her tragic downfall.

MARY: Oh. What happened to her?

MARTA: She fell off the stage.

MARY: What an unlucky thing.

MARTA: Yes, it was by all accounts. She read something, they say, in the mind of an audience volunteer that so startled her, her heart gave way. She plunged over the footlights into the orchestra pit and landed head first in the bell of a tuba.

MARY: She didn't…

MARTA: It really was most unfortunate. You see they couldn't pull her head out of the tuba. And thus, she was buried with it.

MARY: Marta.

MARTA: Oh, yes. The mind of another is a dangerous place.

MARY: You're teasing me.

MARTA: I'm warning you. *(A pause)* Tell me what you want to know.
I'm waiting.

MARY: Well, when you put it like that. I feel on the spot. It seems silly. I don't need to know, really. I don't need to know your full name, birthplace, first language. Your religion, political affiliation, your security clearance— *(She stops herself.)*

MARTA: What is it, Mary?

MARY: I only need to know

MARTA: I'm waiting.

MARY: Why you're here.

MARTA: In the cell, the lice and rats had a feast on me. Left me half-mad and so hungry I chewed my own skin. Nine months of solitary confinement. Like a deadly pregnancy, giving birth to—

MARY: Marta!

MARTA: So, you must understand. That freedom at any cost is preferable.

(End of scene)

Clown Act

(HENRY *as a clown enters playing a toy tuba. He proceeds to perform a silent clown act for a group of children and adults, represented by the audience.*)

(*His act might have something to do with spying and "top secrets" or something altogether different, perhaps a series of magic tricks that fail. As in all clown acts, he seeks connection with the audience, even their participation.*)

(*Most importantly, the act should be touching, funny and ultimately, unsettling.*)

(*End of clown act*)

Scene

(MARTA *and* MARY. *They are looking at photographs. They sit next to each other.*)

MARTA: Is this you?

MARY: Guess again.

MARTA: Your mother?

(MARY *nods her head.*)

MARTA: You look—

MARTA & MARY: —just like her.

MARTA: It's quite striking.

MARY: And a little frightening. (*Showing another photo*)
Here we are together.
She lives near the house now, in a retirement center.
So, I visit her there almost every day. I thought this
would be our chance to finally get to know each other.
Without the distraction of households and men. But
she doesn't want it. Expressly. She's adamant. So, I
stopped trying. The first thing she does when I arrive
is ask about the boys. And so I start to tell her, one son
at a time. And by the fifth one, she is fast asleep. Never
fails. Like clockwork.

(MARTA *and* MARY *laugh.*)

MARTA: So she knows nothing about sons five and six?

MARY: Oh, I change them around. I rotate. Like
yesterday, I started with Rick. The fourth. (*She shows a
photograph and points.*) This is Joe, he's the oldest. That's
Henry, Jr. Then comes Rick, then Larry, Georgie, and
the baby, Jerry. Joe and Rick are starting out in defense.

Larry is a budding prosecutor. Georgie and Jerry are away at school.

MARTA: That leaves Henry, Jr.

MARY: Henry, Jr is finding himself.

MARTA: "Finding himself", I like that.

MARY: "Finding himself", is what he calls it. *(A pause)* And you, Marta?

MARTA: I'm still finding myself, too…

MARY: No. Children, I meant, I wondered if—

MARTA: *(Sharply)* I have one daughter.

MARY: I'm sorry, please—

MARTA: But it's been three years since I last saw her.

MARY: Three years!

MARTA: The three years I've been…traveling.

MARY: Do you have a picture of her?

MARTA: I do, of course. But I never carry it.

MARY: I would so much love to meet her.
One day if, when—

MARTA: It's late. *(She prepares to leave, getting up.)*

MARY: *(Anxiously, stopping her)* Will I see you Saturday?

MARTA: *(Decisively and heavily resuming her seat)* The moment you step out of the house. You never know if you'll see it again. Or anyone. There is no telling. And that's if you're lucky, of course, to have a house. And locks on the door. And no one who pounds on it in the middle of the night. And breaks that door down and carries you off. If you have that, you are luckier than most.

(MARTA and MARY sit awhile.)

MARY: I knew a woman who never left the house.
She worked with Henry at the agency. She was the
last person in the world you would have expected it
from. Outgoing and warm. A terrific secretary and
very beloved. And also respected. She had a lot of
responsibility. And access to information that very few
would ever see. People said that she came to work one
day, as always cheerfully, and began typing something
but then...
She stopped. Something stopped her. She got up, they
say, very calmly, and put the report away. She finished
her other assignments for the rest of the day. And said
goodbye as if nothing had happened. And then she
never came back. And later we heard, she never left the
house.
Some said she simply lost her nerve, became
agoraphobic. Rumors went around that she'd been
unstable for some time and was an alcoholic. Some
attributed it to the woman's change of life.

MARTA: What do you think?

MARY: I think she typed something that she shouldn't
have seen.

MARTA: Something that made her much too
dangerous?

MARY: No, no. She handled top secret files all the time.
The information, I mean.
I think that what she was typing was

MARTA: something you can't expect a person to

MARY: I think it terrified her. Why else would she
never the leave house again?
They hushed it up.

MARTA: What happened to her?

MARY: She died eventually. But several years later.

They took good care of her. Pension, benefits. They kept a good watch on her.

MARTA: I can imagine. Did anyone visit?

MARY: One or two of her closest colleagues. And family. She was divorced, but I did hear the children came occasionally from out of state.

MARTA: How did she seem? What did you hear?

MARY: I heard she seemed broken. She hardly spoke and then in a whisper. And she ate very little. She was a ghost of her former self. They say she wasted away.

(A pause)

MARTA: I wonder what it was, that thing she read.

MARY: It must have been a plan. Or a report. Some form of gathered information. A piece of evidence. In any event, something top secret.

MARTA: A terrible secret.

MARY: I hadn't thought of it in such a long time.

(MARTA and MARY sit in silence for some time.)

(End of scene)

Scene

(HENRY *and* MARTA)

HENRY: How can I thank you for the generous gift? It's priceless and leaves nothing to question.

MARTA: It was a family heirloom. My husband's mother passed it on to us. But my sons have no use for it.

HENRY: It reveals its pleasures only to the specialist.

MARTA: *(Shrugging)* One son plays professional tennis. The other is a bio-chemist.

HENRY: You don't say!

MARTA: I come from a long line of scientists.

HENRY: So, the facts are in your blood.

MARTA: And on my hands. Working for the government. *(A pause)* Blood is hard to wash away.

HENRY: *(Ignoring this)* What excites us the most is its meticulous design. Its thorough, conscientious and efficient construction. In short, it's a thing of beauty whose power overwhelms me and whose meaning we'll uncover more completely over time.
Apropos of time. If you're ever interested in our permanent collection, we would love to invite you to visit. We'll make it very comfortable. There are gorgeous opportunities. Without the risk of forgeries or unfinished business. Whenever you're ready...

MARTA: Thank you, I appreciate it.

HENRY: Meanwhile, funding in the arts continues. A piece of luck, for a cultural attaché. We love new titles and a frame of reference. We love your culture and can't get enough of it.

(HENRY *passes a piece of paper across the table.* MARTA *takes it.*)

HENRY: The museum is open late next week. Think back how short the days were six months ago. And how light the skies will be six days from now.

(*End of scene*)

Scene

(MARY *and* HENRY *in bed. He is sleeping restlessly.*)

MARY: Guess what I did today, Henry? I replaced the toilet roll. Well, we'd run out days ago. It had to be done. I caught a particle of dust on my tongue. And I washed a pair of your underwear. But the stains wouldn't come out down there. So I threw them away. And I found a post-it note in the garbage can. Something about the cultural attaché...

(HENRY *cries out.*)

MARY: So I ground it up and flavored the stew with it.

(HENRY *calms.*)

MARY: That's what I did today.

(HENRY *snuggles against* MARY *in his sleep. She holds him like a mother in her arms.*)

MARY: You're safe. We're safe. It's safe here.

(HENRY *mounts* MARY. *They make love with urgency.*)

(*End of scene*)

Scene

(HENRY, *alone, speaks into the recorder. Package materials at his side.*)

HENRY: Dear Friends. Enclosed, material that should convince you that I remain true and worthy of you. I consider its acquisition to be something of a coup. No one gets near this stuff. And let me warn you up front. It's not for the faint of heart. (*He hesitates, laughs it off, grows serious again.*) Payment might be made in luxury items.

"Thy will be done", (*A pause*) Flash Gordon. (*He stops recorder. Seems to make a decision, then hits record again.*) PS ...Apropos of secrets. A big surprise. Evidence against your "cultural attaché". An irrefutable case of betrayal. These artistic types are so darn fickle. For your information, I have made it known that she is no longer useful to us here. We would be content to see her disappear... (*He stops the recording, pauses. Then almost casually, he takes out tape and wraps it in newspaper, enclosing it in the package as before. He dresses to go out, and whistling, leaves with his package.*)

(*End of scene*)

Scene

(MARTA *and* MARY)

MARY: He's well connected through his family. He's had every advantage. But that can't explain his energy. He pushed ahead. To the top of his profession. His level of responsibility...

MARTA: Yes ...?

MARY: for our security...

MARTA: Is...?

MARY: is very high.

MARTA: How did you meet him?

MARY: Imagine a young girl.

MARTA: I'm imagining, yes.

MARY: Her father worked for the Department of Defense. As did his father, her grandfather on her father's side. And her favorite uncle, her father's brother, he did, too. And now two of six boys. So, it was in the family, you see.

MARTA: And will be...

MARY: For eternity, I guess.

MARTA: And that young girl?

MARY: I joined, too. Just out of high school. I'd won the first prize blue ribbon in my class. For typing.

MARTA: Impressive!

MARY: Yes, I still have it. And so it was clear that I would become a secretary and join that year. I arrived in the capital to take a post. They had special homes then, for girls like us. Alone in the city. I shared a room with another secretary.

MARY: What was she like?

MARY: Just like me.

(MARTA *and* MARY *laugh.*)

MARTA: Where is she now?

MARY: We lost track somehow. But I often think of her. She also married someone inside. That's what you did. We bleached our hair together late one night. And it turned flaming orange!

(MARY *laughs hard—in the memory,* MARTA *joins in.* MARY's *laughter turns to tears.*)

MARY: *(Wiping her eyes)* I'll never forget that as long as I live. We had such laughs. And long, after-midnight talks about the future.

MARTA: *(Gently)* And now here it is. The future you once dreamed about.

(A pause)

MARY: They took good care of us inside. And kept us busy. We attended lectures. We were made to feel part of a very special family. And it was impressed on us how serious our job was and how truly proud we could be. Protecting our national security! The division I was assigned to had a stenographic pool. Thirty girls. There were all sorts of rules.

MARTA: Which division was that?

MARY: Intelligence. I took dictation from the agents. But there were chances for promotion and greater responsibilities...
And so I was promoted to foreign counter intelligence. That's where I met Henry.

When you work in intelligence...

MARTA: So to speak…

MARY: You never admit to it.

MARTA: But everybody knows.

MARY: You just never say it. You work in "defense".

MARTA: "Defense" has the proper resonance.

MARY: He has access to the most sensitive information
and a large array of clearances.

MARTA: And no friend in the world he can share it
with.

MARY: No. No one.

MARTA: That must be very lonely for him.

MARY: It destroys you from the outside in. And then
the damage spreads… *(A pause)* My grandfather on
my mother's side was a wood carver. He left his home
in the Black Forest and made his way over. In the city,
he built tables and beds and cupboards for a living. A
thriving profession in a city of immigrants, setting up
house here for the first time. And on his days off. He
carved. Wild flowers and forest creatures. Mystical
beings. Fantastic to look at. With incredible eyes. He
claimed he had caught them. Back home in the forest.
And I believed him, of course. They scared me to
death. But I couldn't take my eyes off them.
And he read palms. Became famous for it. In our
neighborhood. And he taught me.
Let me see your palm.

*(MARTA gives MARY her hand. MARY takes it in hers, rubs
it gently, and then begins to study it.)*

MARTA: Well?

(MARY says nothing.)

MARTA: What does it say?

(MARY *doesn't answer. Something appears to have stunned her and confirmed something in her mind. But she shrugs and shakes her head.*)

MARY: If you believe it or not, I've forgotten how.

(MARY *continues to hold* MARTA'*s hand.*)

(*End of scene*)

Scene

(MARY *and* HENRY. *They are in bed. He is sleeping.*)

MARY: Henry? Father Joseph paid a call today. Wanted
to know how we were getting on. Said he hadn't seen
us in a while. And he asked about the boys, as usual.
Then he asked me if I was feeling all right. Said he
noticed a change in me. "Change," I said, "What do
you mean, Father?" "Mary, I can't say for sure," he
said. "I'm no mind-reader. Is anything troubling you?"

(HENRY *begins to thrash around and wince and shudder in
his sleep.* MARY *watches him.*)

MARY: There are no secrets that Father doesn't hear.
How does he hold them all? Well, he can't. It's not
possible...
He passes them on. (*She watches him.*) To the highest
authority.

(HENRY *cries out in his sleep.*)

MARY: (*Quickly, to him*) To God, I mean...

(*End of scene*)

Scene

(HENRY, *alone, speaks into recorder. Package materials near him*)

HENRY: Dear Friends. You ask me quite correctly, to look out for my safety. I am deeply touched. Although we have never met, I feel you above all others understand me.

What I am sharing with you now. (*He stops recording. He appears to be sweating and is having troubling speaking. He takes a deep breath in and out. And then he starts recording again.*) What I am sharing with you now... (*Again, he stops recording, seeks composure, and then starts again.*) What I am sharing with you now...to all extents and purposes...is outside the boundaries of knowledge and sense.

And should we not live well in spite of this?

Thank you for the watches.

Cash is acceptable and again desirable. (*He pauses, stops recorder, thinks, hits record again. Slowly*) By the way, today I had the funny feeling that I was being tailed. And it occurred to me that you may not have been able to contain your curiosity. As to who I am. Such a development would wound me greatly. I stand by our intimate anonymity. Yours in trust?

Uncle Sam... (*He smiles, stops the recorder.*) King Kong!... (*He beats his chest and bellows like a gorilla. He laughs, but then begins to breathe heavily and to shake. After a time, he takes out the tape and inserts it into the package, whistling. But he does not leave. He sits back. He studies the package on his desk for some time, then fingers it, turning it this way and that.*)

(*End of scene*)

Scene

(The living room. MARY, HENRY *and* MARTA*)*

MARTA: I have to congratulate you on the renovation of your kitchen!

HENRY: Granite and steel.

MARTA: Ideal. For cooking *and* cleaning.

MARY: Not even nuclear war could destroy it.

MARTA: Or the next great flood…
But now I am afraid I have to say goodbye.

MARY & HENRY: "Goodbye"?

MARY: Marta! Why?

MARTA: Sudden pressing mission, and I'm called back. That taken care of, off I'm sent again. Art is never a long-term priority.

HENRY: Out of six sons, we've got one artistic one. And he's the son that worries me. But Mary encourages his eccentricities.

MARY: *(Ignoring him)* Sent where?

MARTA: Oh, that's never clear. In the cultural field…

HENRY: —We're certainly going to miss having you with us. It's been both a cultural and *personal* bonus. Hasn't it, Mary…?

MARY: When are you leaving?

MARTA: Late this evening.

HENRY: So soon!

MARTA: It's always short notice.

MARY: *(Almost in a whisper)* What time are you flying out?

MARTA: Scheduled departure is 10pm. It was so lovely to visit again. By the way, the guard knew me at the gate.

HENRY: How'd you like that!

MARTA: Felt like I knew him, too. Seen him before. More than once in fact...

HENRY: A guardian angel, maybe?

MARTA: *(To him)* I expect we all need someone like that. *(Getting up and taking her leave)* Mary. Such a tasty last supper.

(They shake hands rather formally.)

HENRY: *(Bowing out of the room)* While you say goodbye, I'll call for your car.

(Left alone, MARTA and MARY move together.)

MARY: Don't go, Marta.

MARTA: It's not in my power to say no.

MARY: I won't say goodbye.

MARTA: Yes. Saying goodbye is a fallacy.

(MARY does not respond.)

MARTA: Because what does it mean, anyway?

(MARY remains silent, unable to speak.)

MARTA: I knew a woman—

MARY: *Don't.* Not now.

(MARTA and MARY embrace.)

MARTA: —who never said "goodbye". She'd just up and leave. Leave you speechless there. In mid-sentence, mid-meal, mid-air.
As if she'd never been.

(MARTA *releases herself from their embrace and leaves*
abruptly without another word. The sound of a car door
slamming and a car starting up is heard. MARY *goes to the*
window and watches.)

(*End of scene*)

Home Movie

(A black stage. A video with sound is being screened on a wall. It has the feel of a home movie. And there is clearly someone unseen controlling its play. Scenes we have been watching replay like a montage but filmed in the real world not on a stage, sometimes paused for a moment, sometimes fast forwarded, other times rewound. Scenes between the three characters; ; between MARTA and MARY; between MARTA and HENRY; HENRY alone; between MARY and HENRY in bed. The video ends with MARY and MARTA embracing and holds this image for some time.)

(End of home movie)

Scene

(HENRY, *alone, speaks into his recorder. There is no package.*)

HENRY: *(Bravely)* Dear Friends. *(He grows serious.)* No response from you. No answer to my signals. Not hearing leaves me edgy. I hate silence.
Particularly troubling is the reneging on payment. *(He does not move. The recorder continues to play.)*

(End of scene)

Scene

(MARY *and* HENRY *in bed. He is sleeping.*)

MARY: Have you heard anything from the cultural attaché? Henry? How many days is it since she left? One, two, three…five six seven.

Do you remember the old days, Henry? "Loyalty was a quiet love of country and a pride in its ideals which all men carried in their hearts." (*She looks at him.*) You've sold her and shipped her back for payment. And for seven days, she has been interrogated …

(MARTA's *voice is heard. She is present but not visible.*)

MARTA: It is so still here. Nothing moves. Nothing. I don't know where I am. I'm blindfolded. So I can't see anything except a tiny patch of earth below my feet. There is a tiny flower pushing out of the ground. A wildflower. My own garden. The garden of Eden? I believe it's morning. Last night, I heard a harp on the wind. Or was it a hawk circling? I see my father coming in the door. Home again. We're safe. I feel his rough beard against my cheek. I see my mother in the kitchen. Her strong hands covered in flour, against an apron bursting with poppies. I am in her arms, on her warm heaving breast, smelling of good bread. I've not eaten. I've not slept. Stars are bursting behind my eyes. Every morning, I am given a glass of water which tastes like the earth and I am a part of it already. My veins fill like rivers and my cells open receiving one more day of life. I can't remember my name. I see a woman's face. She is crying.

(MARY *covers her face with her hands.*)

MARTA: But I can't lift my arms to comfort her. They are bound behind my back. And my feet are bound. When I collapse, two strong arms prop me back up. I've come to love those arms. Their power. And I trust them to be there when I fall again.
We children are playing in a field. Laughing and screaming and whispering secrets to one another. No. Stop. Someone is whispering in my ear. I think it is the man with the strong arms. But I can't hear what he is saying.
I feel his breath on my ear. It is smoky, not unpleasant. What does he want from me? That I have not given him already? That I would not give again for a piece of bread? A place to lie down?
Wait! He is removing the blindfold from my eyes! And the shackles from my ankles, my hands. And gently pushing me. I falter. I cannot see. I do not feel my arms. My legs. But like a miracle, I am running.

(A single shot rings out.)

MARY: *(Suddenly)* What did Marta say about the children's game? The terrible secret, Henry. Could it not, in fact, be its opposite? A revelation that would change the world for the better?

(Sound of the front door being broken down. HENRY jolts up. MARY smiles.)

MARY: The most wondrous arrival of our savior?

(The bedroom door is kicked down.)

(End of scene)

END OF PLAY